Quick & Simple Sides

W9-CEX-898

Easy accompaniments to any meal

easy cheesy potatoes

PREP: 15 min. | TOTAL: 1 hour 10 min. | MAKES: 10 servings, ½ cup each.

▶ what you need!

1 lb. russet potatoes (about 4 medium), cut into ½-inch chunks

½ lb. (8 oz.) VELVEETA Pasteurized Prepared Cheese Product, cut up

½ cup chopped onions

¼ cup KRAFT Real Mayo Mayonnaise

4 slices OSCAR MAYER Bacon, cooked, drained and crumbled (about ¼ cup)

▶ make it!

HEAT oven to 375°F.

1. **COMBINE** all ingredients except bacon in 8-inch square baking dish sprayed with cooking spray; cover with foil.

2. **BAKE** 45 min.

3. **TOP** with bacon; bake, uncovered, 5 to 10 min. or until potatoes are tender.

corn souffle

PREP: 15 min. | TOTAL: 55 min. | MAKES: 16 servings.

▶ what you need!

2 Tbsp. butter

1 pkg. (8 oz.) PHILADELPHIA Cream Cheese, cubed

1 can (15¼ oz.) whole kernel corn, drained

1 can (14.75 oz.) cream-style corn

1 pkg. (8.5 oz.) corn muffin mix

2 eggs, beaten

1 cup KRAFT Shredded Cheddar Cheese

▶ make it!

HEAT oven to 350°F.

1. **MICROWAVE** butter in medium microwaveable bowl on HIGH 30 sec. or until melted. Stir in cream cheese. Microwave 15 sec. or until cream cheese is softened; stir until cream cheese is completely melted and mixture is well blended. Add next 4 ingredients; mix well.

2. **POUR** into 13×9-inch pan sprayed with cooking spray; top with Cheddar.

3. **BAKE** 40 min. or until golden brown. Cool slightly.

SERVING SUGGESTION:
This dish is versatile enough to pair with your favorite barbecued meat, beef stew, chicken soup or even chili.

SUBSTITUTE:
Prepare using PHILADELPHIA Neufchâtel Cheese.

SPECIAL EXTRA:
Add 2 sliced green onions along with the corns, muffin mix and eggs.

MEXICAN-STYLE CORN SOUFFLE:
Prepare as directed, substituting 1 can (11 oz.) whole kernel corn with chopped red and green peppers for the plain whole kernel corn.

creamy vegetable bake

PREP: 20 min. | TOTAL: 50 min. | MAKES: 10 servings, ¾ cup each.

▸ what you need!

1 pkg. (8 oz.) PHILADELPHIA Cream Cheese, softened

⅓ cup milk

¼ cup KRAFT Grated Parmesan Cheese

1 tsp. dried basil leaves

4 large carrots, diagonally sliced

½ lb. sugar snap peas

½ lb. fresh asparagus, cut into 1-inch lengths

1 large red bell pepper, chopped

1 pkg. (6 oz.) STOVE TOP Stuffing Mix for Chicken

▸ make it!

HEAT oven to 350°F.

1. **MICROWAVE** cream cheese and milk in large microwaveable bowl on HIGH 1 min. or until cream cheese is melted and mixture is blended when stirred. Add Parmesan and basil; stir until blended. Add vegetables; toss to coat.

2. **SPOON** into greased 13×9-inch baking dish. Prepare stuffing as directed on package; spoon over vegetable mixture.

3. **BAKE** 30 min. or until golden brown.

SUBSTITUTE:
Prepare using PHILADELPHIA Neufchâtel Cheese.

HOW TO SELECT SUGAR SNAP PEAS:
Sugar snap peas are a cross between the common English pea and snow peas. Both the pod and the peas inside are edible. Choose pods that are plump, crisp and bright green. Before using, snap off the stem ends, pulling to remove any strings.

easy cheesy scalloped potatoes

PREP: 30 min. | TOTAL: 1 hour 30 min. | MAKES: 15 servings, ¾ cup each.

▶ what you need!

1 pkg. (8 oz.) PHILADELPHIA Cream Cheese, softened

½ cup BREAKSTONE'S or KNUDSEN Sour Cream

1 cup chicken broth

3 lb. red potatoes (about 9), thinly sliced

1 pkg. (6 oz.) OSCAR MAYER Smoked Ham, chopped

1 pkg. (8 oz.) KRAFT Shredded Cheddar Cheese, divided

1 cup frozen peas

▶ make it!

HEAT oven to 350°F.

1. **MIX** cream cheese, sour cream and broth in large bowl until well blended. Add potatoes, ham, 1¾ cups Cheddar and peas; stir gently to evenly coat all ingredients.

2. **SPOON** into 13×9-inch baking dish sprayed with cooking spray; top with remaining Cheddar.

3. **BAKE** 1 hour or until casserole is heated through and potatoes are tender.

SERVING SUGGESTION:
Balance this creamy, indulgent side dish by serving it alongside cooked lean meat or fish and a steamed green vegetable.

PURCHASING POTATOES:
Look for firm, smooth, well-shaped potatoes that are free of wrinkles, cracks and blemishes. Avoid any with green-tinged skins or sprouting "eyes" or buds.

VARIATION:
Substitute OSCAR MAYER Smoked Turkey for the ham and/or 1 cup frozen mixed vegetables for the peas.

crust topped broccoli cheese bake

PREP: 10 min. | TOTAL: 40 min. | MAKES: 14 servings.

▶ what you need!

½ cup (½ of 8-oz. tub) PHILADELPHIA Chive & Onion Cream Cheese Spread

1 can (10¾ oz.) condensed cream of mushroom soup

½ cup water

2 pkg. (16 oz. each) frozen broccoli florets, thawed, drained

1 cup KRAFT Shredded Cheddar Cheese

1 thawed frozen puff pastry sheet (½ of 17.3-oz. pkg.)

1 egg, beaten

▶ make it!

HEAT oven to 400°F.

1. **MIX** cream cheese spread, soup and water in large bowl until well blended. Stir in broccoli and Cheddar. Spoon into 2½- to 3-qt. shallow rectangular or oval baking dish.

2. **ROLL** pastry sheet on lightly floured surface to fit top of baking dish. Cover dish completely with pastry. Press pastry edges against rim of dish to seal. Brush with egg; pierce with knife to vent.

3. **BAKE** 30 min. or until filling is heated through and pastry is puffed and golden brown.

MAKE AHEAD:
Casserole can be assembled in advance. Refrigerate up to 24 hours. When ready to serve, bake (uncovered) as directed.

VARIATION:
Prepare as directed, using PHILADELPHIA Chive & Onion ⅓ Less Fat than Cream Cheese and KRAFT 2% Milk Shredded Cheddar Cheese.

easy risotto with bacon & peas

PREP: 10 min. | TOTAL: 40 min. | MAKES: 6 servings, 1 cup each.

▶ what you need!

6 slices OSCAR MAYER Bacon, cut into 1-inch pieces

1 onion, chopped

1½ cups medium grain rice, uncooked

2 cloves garlic, minced

3 cans (15 oz. each) chicken broth

4 oz. (½ of 8-oz. pkg.) PHILADELPHIA Cream Cheese, cubed

1 cup frozen peas, thawed

2 Tbsp. chopped fresh parsley

2 Tbsp. KRAFT Grated Parmesan Cheese, divided

▶ make it!

1. **COOK** bacon and onions in large skillet on medium-high heat 5 min. or just until bacon is crisp, stirring occasionally.

2. **ADD** rice and garlic; cook 3 min. or until rice is opaque, stirring frequently. Gradually add ½ can broth, cook and stir 3 min. or until broth is completely absorbed. Repeat with remaining broth, adding the cream cheese with the last addition of broth and cooking 5 min. or until the cream cheese is completely melted and mixture is well blended.

3. **STIR** in peas; cook 2 min. or until peas are heated through, stirring occasionally. Remove from heat. Stir in parsley and 1 Tbsp. Parmesan. Serve topped with remaining Parmesan.

SUBSTITUTE:
Prepare using fat-free reduced-sodium chicken broth.

SERVING SUGGESTION:
Serve with hot crusty bread and a mixed green salad topped with your favorite KRAFT Dressing.

garlic mashed potatoes

▶ what you need!

2½ lb. potatoes (about 7), peeled, quartered

4 cloves garlic, minced

1 tub (8 oz.) PHILADELPHIA Cream Cheese Spread

1 Tbsp. butter or margarine

1 tsp. salt

▶ make it!

1. **COOK** potatoes and garlic in boiling water in large saucepan 20 min. or until potatoes are tender; drain.

2. **MASH** potatoes until smooth.

3. **STIR** in remaining ingredients until well blended.

SERVING SUGGESTION:
Add contrast to the potatoes by serving them with a crisp mixed green salad or vegetable, and lean fish, meat or poultry.

FOOD FACTS:
For best results, use russet or red potatoes since they work best for mashing.

SUBSTITUTE:
Prepare using PHILADELPHIA Chive & Onion Cream Cheese Spread.

MAKE IT EASY:
Use mixer to beat potatoes instead of using a hand masher.

zucchini with parmesan sauce

▶ what you need!

3 zucchini (1 lb.), cut diagonally into ½-inch-thick slices

2 yellow squash, cut diagonally into ½-inch-thick slices

1 red onion, cut into wedges

1 Tbsp. oil

1 tub (8 oz.) PHILADELPHIA Chive & Onion Cream Cheese Spread

⅓ cup fat-free milk

¼ cup KRAFT Grated Parmesan Cheese

¼ tsp. herb and spice blend seasoning

▶ make it!

1. **COOK** and stir vegetables in hot oil in large skillet 5 to 7 min. or until crisp-tender.

2. **MEANWHILE,** place remaining ingredients in small saucepan; cook on low heat until cream cheese spread is completely melted and mixture is well blended and heated through, stirring occasionally.

3. **SERVE** sauce over vegetables.

HEALTHY LIVING:
Save 4 grams of fat per serving by preparing with PHILADELPHIA Chive & Onion ⅓ Less Fat than Cream Cheese.

oat-topped sweet potato crisp

PREP: 20 min. | TOTAL: 1 hour | MAKES: 8 servings.

▸ what you need!

1 pkg. (8 oz.) PHILADELPHIA Cream Cheese, softened

1 can (40 oz.) cut sweet potatoes, drained

¾ cup packed brown sugar, divided

¼ tsp. ground cinnamon

1 Granny Smith apple, chopped

⅔ cup chopped cranberries

½ cup flour

½ cup old-fashioned or quick-cooking oats, uncooked

⅓ cup cold butter or margarine

¼ cup chopped PLANTERS Pecans

▸ make it!

HEAT oven to 350°F.

1. **BEAT** cream cheese, potatoes, ¼ cup sugar and cinnamon with mixer until well blended. Spoon into 1½-qt. casserole; top with apples and cranberries.

2. **MIX** flour, oats and remaining sugar in medium bowl; cut in butter until mixture resembles coarse crumbs. Stir in nuts. Sprinkle over fruit layer in casserole.

3. **BAKE** 35 to 40 min. or until heated through.

SUBSTITUTE:
Prepare using PHILADELPHIA Neufchâtel Cheese.

broccoli & cauliflower supreme

PREP: 25 min. | TOTAL: 25 min. | MAKES: 6 servings.

▶ what you need!

4 oz. (½ of 8-oz. pkg.) PHILADELPHIA Fat Free Cream Cheese, cubed

¼ cup KRAFT FREE Peppercorn Ranch Dressing

1 Tbsp. GREY POUPON Dijon Mustard

1½ bunches broccoli, cut into florets (about 6 cups), steamed, drained

½ head cauliflower, cut into florets (about 3 cups), steamed, drained

12 RITZ Reduced Fat Crackers, crushed (about ½ cup)

▶ make it!

1. **MICROWAVE** cream cheese, dressing and mustard in medium microwaveable bowl on HIGH 30 to 45 sec. or until cream cheese is softened and sauce is heated through. Stir until cream cheese is completely melted and sauce is well blended.

2. **COMBINE** vegetables in large bowl. Add sauce; toss until vegetables are evenly coated.

3. **TRANSFER** to serving bowl; top with cracker crumbs.

SUBSTITUTE:
Prepare using frozen broccoli and cauliflower florets.

NUTRITION BONUS:
Delight your family with this creamy and delicious, yet low-fat side dish that is high in both vitamins A and C from the broccoli.

cheesy rice & corn casserole

PREP: 10 min. | TOTAL: 35 min. | MAKES: 8 servings, ½ cup each.

▶ what you need!

½ cup (½ of 8-oz. tub) PHILADELPHIA Chive & Onion Cream Cheese Spread

1 egg

2 cups cooked instant white rice

1 can (15¼ oz.) corn with red and green bell peppers, drained

1 cup KRAFT Mexican Style Finely Shredded Four Cheese, divided

2 Tbsp. chopped fresh cilantro

▶ make it!

HEAT oven to 375°F.

1. **MIX** cream cheese spread and egg in large bowl until well blended. Stir in rice, corn, ¾ cup shredded cheese and cilantro.

2. **POUR** into greased 1½-qt. casserole; top with remaining shredded cheese.

3. **BAKE** 20 to 25 min. or until casserole is heated through and cheese is melted.

SPECIAL EXTRA:
Add 1 to 2 tsp. ground cumin for more Mexican flavor.

5-minute cheesy broccoli toss

PREP: 5 min. | TOTAL: 10 min. | MAKES: 4 servings, about ¾ cup each.

▶ what you need!

4 cups frozen broccoli florets

½ tsp. dry mustard

¼ lb. (4 oz.) VELVEETA Pasteurized Prepared Cheese Product, cut into ½-inch cubes

1 Tbsp. KRAFT Grated Parmesan Cheese

▶ make it!

1. **COMBINE** broccoli, mustard and VELVEETA in large nonstick skillet on medium-high heat.

2. **COOK** 5 min. or until broccoli is crisp-tender and mixture is heated through, stirring occasionally.

3. **SPRINKLE** with Parmesan.

SPECIAL EXTRA:
Add 1 minced garlic clove with the broccoli.

bacon-spinach bites

PREP: 10 min. | TOTAL: 30 min. | MAKES: 12 servings.

▶ what you need!

4 oz. (½ of 8-oz. pkg.) PHILADELPHIA Cream Cheese, softened

4 green onions, sliced

1 pkg. (10 oz.) frozen chopped spinach, thawed, squeezed dry

6 slices OSCAR MAYER Bacon, cooked, crumbled

3 Tbsp. flour

4 eggs, beaten

¼ lb. (4 oz.) VELVEETA Pasteurized Prepared Cheese Product, cut into 12 cubes

▶ make it!

HEAT oven to 350°F.

1. **MIX** cream cheese and onions in medium bowl. Add spinach, bacon and flour; mix well. Stir in eggs.

2. **SPOON** into 12 greased and floured muffin pan cups. Top each with 1 VELVEETA cube; press gently into center of filling.

3. **BAKE** 20 min. or until centers are set and tops are golden brown. Serve warm or chilled.

MINIATURE BACON-SPINACH BITES:
Prepare spinach mixture as directed; spoon into 24 greased and floured miniature muffin pan cups. Cut VELVEETA into 24 cubes; press 1 into batter in each cup. Bake 14 to 16 min. or until centers are set and tops are golden brown. Makes 12 servings, 2 bites each.